Pebble Bilingual Books

El agua como líquido/

Water as a Liquid

de/by
Helen Frost

Traducción/Translation
Martín Luis Guzmán Ferrer, Ph.D.

Capstone Press
Mankato, Minnesota

Pebble Bilingual Books are published by Capstone Press
151 Good Counsel Drive, P.O. Box 669, Mankato, Minnesota 56002
http://www.capstone-press.com

1 2 3 4 5 6 08 07 06 05 04 03

Library of Congress Cataloging-in-Publication Data
Frost, Helen, 1949–
   [Water as a liquid. Spanish & English.]
   El agua como líquido / de Helen frost; traduccíon, Martín Luis Guzmán Ferrer = Water as a
liquid / by Helen Frost; translation, Martín Luis Guzmán Ferrer.
   p. cm.—(Pebble Bilingual Books)
   Text in Spanish and English.
   Summary: Simple text presents facts about water in its liquid state, where it is found, and
some of its properties.
   ISBN 0-7368-2312-3 (hardcover)
   1. Water—Juvenile literature. [1. Water. 2. Spanish language materials—Bilingual.]
   I. Title: Water as a liquid. II. Title.
GB662.3 .F7613 2004
551.46—dc21   2002156393

Editorial Credits
Mari C. Schuh and Martha E. H. Rustad, editors; Timothy Halldin, cover designer; Linda Clavel,
   interior designer; Patrick Dentinger, cover production designer; Kimberly Danger, photo
   researcher; María Fiol, Spanish copy editor; Gail Saunders-Smith, consulting editor; Carolyn M.
   Tucker, Water Education Specialist, California Department of Water Resources, reviewer

Photo Credits
Cheryl A. Ertelt, 14; ColePhoto/Robin Cole, 10; David F. Clobes, 18; Index Stock Imagery/Carmen
Northern (1989), 16; International Stock/Art Brewer, cover; James P. Rowan, 8; John Elk III, 4;
Photri-Microstock/Novastock, 6; Richard Hamilton Smith, 12; Robert McCaw, 1, 20

Special thanks to:
• Isabel Schon, Ph.D., director of the Barahona Center for the Study of Books in Spanish for
  Children and Adolescents, San Marcos, California, for her assistance in preparing the Spanish
  portion of this book.
• Mike Lundgren, science teacher at Fairmont High School in Fairmont, Minnesota, for his helpful
  assistance with the English content of this book.

Table of Contents

Contenido

4

Water can be a solid,
a gas, or a liquid. Water
is a liquid when it is not
too cold or too warm.

El agua puede ser sólido, gas
o líquido. El agua es un
líquido cuando no está ni
muy fría ni muy caliente.

Water as a liquid
does not have a shape.
It is the shape of
whatever holds it.

El agua como líquido
no tiene forma. Tiene
la forma de aquello
que la contiene.

Clouds are dust and
tiny drops of water.
Sometimes the water falls
to the ground as rain.

Las nubes son de polvo y
gotitas de agua. Algunas
veces el agua cae sobre
la tierra como lluvia.

Some water goes into
the ground. People pump
groundwater from wells.

El agua puede entrar
en la tierra. La gente bombea
esa agua de los pozos.

Some water fills
lakes and rivers.

El agua puede llenar
los lagos y los ríos.

Water flows from high places
to low places. Rivers carry
water to oceans.

El agua corre de los lugares
altos a los lugares bajos.
Los ríos llevan el agua
al mar.

Most water on the earth
is in oceans. Water in
oceans is salt water.
Salt water is not safe
for people to drink.

La mayor parte del agua
de la Tierra está en el mar.
El agua de mar es agua
salada. El agua salada no
es buena para beber.

Water in most rivers
and lakes is freshwater.
People and animals need
freshwater to drink.

El agua en la mayoría de los
ríos y lagos es agua dulce.
Las personas y los animales
deben beber agua limpia.

Water is a part of all living things. People, plants, and animals need water to live.

El agua es parte de todos los seres vivientes. La gente, las plantas y los animales necesitan del agua para vivir.

Glossary

freshwater—water without salt in it; water from the faucet is freshwater.

groundwater—water that is found underground; groundwater can be pumped from wells.

liquid—a substance that flows freely; a liquid does not have a shape; water is a liquid between 32 degrees Fahrenheit and 212 degrees Fahrenheit (0 degrees Celsius and 100 degrees Celsius).

ocean—a very large body of water; most water on the earth is in oceans.

pump—to force a liquid from one place into another place using a machine

salt water—water with a lot of salt in it; water in oceans is salt water; salt water is not safe for people to drink.

well—a deep hole in the ground out of which people pump water

Glosario

agua dulce *(la)*—agua que no tiene sal; el agua de la llave es dulce.

agua de pozo *(la)*—el agua que se encuentra bajo tierra; el agua de pozo se bombea de los pozos.

líquido *(el)*—una sustancia que corre libremente; un líquido no tiene forma; el agua es un líquido entre los 0 y los 100 grados Celsius (32 y 212 grados Fahrenheit).

mar *(el)*—un cuerpo de agua muy grande; la mayoría del agua de la Tierra se encuentra en los mares.

bombear—forzar un líquido a pasar de un lugar a otro empleando una máquina

agua salada *(la)*—agua que tiene mucha sal; el agua de mar es salada; a la gente le hace daño beber agua salada.

pozo *(el)*—un hoyo muy hondo en la tierra de donde la gente bombea agua

Index

Índice

DATE DUE